EASY SHORT ORGAN PIECES IN EASY KEYS

BOOK II

Noel Jones, AAGO · EDITOR

SACRED MUSIC LIBRARY

SACRED MUSIC LIBRARY
Augusta, Kentucky

WWW. SACREDMUSICLIBRARY.COM

Introduction

These pieces are short in most cases, but it is simple to change to a different keyboard or a different stop setting and you are encouraged to play the second time more softly. Repetition is a wonderful thing to hear when it is slightly different.

Organ music for the Mass has to be like vocal music for the Mass, not distracting but creative with the harmonies and expression. Organ builders describe the sound of different pipes as vowels.

The earliest organ music was played without expression (getting louder and softer) as the Swell shades, usually wooden shutters, control the loudness and timbre of the sound of the pipes that are in large wooden boxes. They were first invented at the time of Bach, but it is doubtful he ever played an organ with them.

When they open more sound is heard and this can also be brighter.

You will find that there are times that playing legato, very smooth connecting notes that follow each note, is the prime job of the organ. However, you will have times when you need to "articulate", meaning a bit of air in between playing notes.

Playing anything fast during the Mass is also distracting, though before and especially after Mass that may be done.

The organ pieces in this volume are taken from books in the Catholic Organist's Quarterly Series that are almost all Manuals Only and each book including different levels of difficulty. As we work on the series, we find that there is special need of easy music in easy keys to assemble these books to build confidence in new organists.

This series now includes:
Very Easy Preludes on Hymns for Solo Stops or Chimes
Easy Organ Music in Easy Keys for Mass
A Catholic Book of Hymns ~ Vol. V Simple Organ Edition

CONTENTS

Easy Organ Pieces from THE CATHOLIC ORGANIST'S QUARTERLY – SUMMER

Easy Organ Pieces from THE CATHOLIC ORGANIST'S QUARTERLY – MARIAN ORGAN MUSIC

Easy Organ Pieces from A CATHOLIC ORGANIST'S BOOK OF PRELUDES FOR ORGAN

Easy Organ Pieces from A CATHOLIC ORGANIST'S BOOK OF OFFERTORY & COMMUNION MUSIC FOR ORGAN

Playing Notes

Elevation — A. Guilmant, 1837–1911
This piece could be played on Full Organ with the expression pedals set to their softest level, then increasing slightly following the expression signs in the music and decreasing, creating a very majestic sound. This piece may also be played on the softest stops on the organ.

Benedicamus Domino — J.-N. Lemmens, 1823–1881
Fughetta - Orbis Factor
An 8' Principal with a 2/3' Twelfth come to mind as a full stop with the mutation, the 12th, addin an edge to the sound.

Toccata — J. C. Bach, 1735–1782
Play only the lower of the octaves in the left hand—this could be played on the harpsichord—where the octaves would be helpful, but the steady tone of the lower note is enough on the organ. Choose light and bright stops!

Thanks Be to God — S. Ochs, 1858–1929
This piece lends itself to 8' and 4' stops but feel free to add others to fill your church with sound.

Von Himmel Hoch — J. G. Walther, 1687–1748
Very bright and light stops, with a zimbelstern or, if this is being played outside of Mass, borrow the Sanctus bells and have someone ring them near the organ, and be very sure to put them back!

In Dulci Jubilo — J. M. Bach, 1648–1694
Clear 8' and 4' stops, with a light 16' pedal stop on as well. You have two feet. Use the right foot to play the tied G until measure 25, D at measure 27, release at measure 61, then play the G on measure 70.

Ave Maris Stella — F. Benoist, 1794–1878
Use 8' Principal with other stops, to hear the melodic lines against each other. If you play pedals, play the bass line using a 8' reed in the pedal division or coupled from a manual. If you do not play the pedals, set the stops in the same way and use the Bass Coupler which will play the lowest note on the great for you in the pedals.

Grand Choeur — M.-A. Charpentier, 1643–1704
Grand Choeur on a French organ is usually the term for full organ. However, bear in mind that the full organ of Charpentier's day was quite different from the full organ of an organ built today. There was also a principle of registering that is not the same as our idea today. Avoid 16' tone altogether, as there were very few 16' stops on French Baroque organs. When building the chorus avoid heavy principals and mixtures. Use quiet flue and flute stops with reeds at 8' for an authentic sound. Some mutations can add character to the sound without overwhelming it.

Quiet Prelude on MAGI — N. Jones, b. 1947
Noel Jones has written a masterful prelude on this well-known tune that would be perfect for an Epiphany prelude. I would choose clear, quiet stops, without using undulating stops (strings).

Da Jesus an dem Kreuze stund — S. Scheidt, 1587–1654
Chorale
As you are not accompanying a congregation with this chorale, there is no need to register it as if it was a hymn. Instead, I would use 8' and 4' principals to give weight without volume.

VI me Messe — C. Justin, ca. 1830–ca. 1873
After the Epistle
Plein Jeu differs from the Grand Jeu. It is closer in style and composition to our modern principal chorus. Use 8', 4', and 2' principals with a sharp mixture (or the brightest and highest pitched one you have available).

Asperges Me — J. Diebold, 1842–1929
As this is supposed to be an introduction to chant, I would use quiet, clear stops like flutes.

Kyrie Eleison — L. Perosi, 1872–1956
Quiet principal stops would work beautifully on this piece: perhaps 8' and 4' principals on the Swell or Choir.

Regina Cæli — M. Corrette, 1707–1795
Antiphon: Use an 8' reed for the Cantus Firmus in the Left Hand, accompanied by 8' and 4' flues on the Right Hand.

Rondeau — J. Duphly, 1715–1789
Utilize a "fond orgue" sound for this work: quieter 8' and 4' principals.

Cantilena — O. Ravanello, 1871–1938
Slowly this is like a chant of 4 measures that builds and falls. 8' stops with a warm sound work well. Move ahead a bit moved, but then back to the slow, almost rocking, theme throughout.

Vorspiel zu: Ecce Panis Angelorum — J. Diebold, 1842–1929
This could be played quietly or loudly. Allow yourself the freedom to experiment with a variety of sounds to determine which ones you like.

Benediction — L. J. A. Lefébure-Wély, 1817–1869
Use 8' and 4' or 8', 4', and 2' flutes.

Fughetta — A. Scarlatti, 1660–1725
8', 4', and 2' flutes would be perfect for this beautiful Fughetta by Scarlatti.

Fugue — A. M. Panseron, 1756–1859
This sould be registered with a large principal chorus and mixture, as an impressive fugue for a postlude (no 16' tone should be used, as it muddies the texture).

Fuga Sesta — G. P. Telemann, 1681–1767
This fugue would work extremely well as an impressive postlude, in which case you would want to use a principal chorus and mixture.

Basse de Trompette — L. Marchand, 1669–1732
Use a solo 8' trumpet in the Left Hand, with an 8' and 4' combination in the Right Hand that will balance against it without overpowering it.

Rigaudon — G. Böhm, 1661–1733
Use a solo trumpet stop in the Right Hand, and a principal chorus in the Left Hand that balances with it. This principal chorus will also be used in the Right Hand in the sections that are not intended for solo trumpet.

Offertorio — J.-F. Dandrieu, c. 1682–1738
This is one of those pieces that can be played convincingly on either a soft or loud registration. Stay away from 16' stops, and always strive for clarity in the sound, even when it's louder. Mixtures and reeds are always appropriate in French baroque organ music.

Herr Jesu Christ dich zu uns wend — GP Telemann, 1681–1767
Flutes at 8', 4', and 2', or just at 8' and 2' would give this piece the sparkle and excitement that it calls for.

Basse de Trompette — J.-F. Dandrieu, c. 1682–1738
The registration is clearly laid out at the beginning of this piece. A trumpet solo in the bass, with "sweet" sounds in the right hand. Obviously choose stops that will balance the trumpet without overpowering it. Note that this piece would probably have been played with notes inégales, a wide spread practice in the French Baroque period where the eighth notes would have been played with a swing rather than evenly: try the eighth note passages this way and see if you like the results.

Christ Ist Erstanden — *Buxheimer Orgelbuch*, 1460
There are a number of ways you could treat this piece, but one of the most exciting would be to play it on just 8' reeds. Couple all the 8' chorus reeds on the organ (avoid any solo reeds, such as a Festival Trumpet), and see if you like the sound. It has a quality to it that works very well in the late medieval music like this. You can adjust the combination until you find one you like.

Komm, Heiliger Geist — G. P. Telemann, 1681–1767
While this piece could be played on one manual only, it would certainly sound great on two, with the chorale melody on the right hand played on an impressive solo stop and the accompaniment on a balancing chorus underneath.

Veni Creator III — J. Titelouze, 1563–1633 74
These pieces were originally written to be played in between verses of the hymn. This was a tradition that was strong in France at the time Titelouze wrote this piece. The registration of the versets would reflect, in some sense, the words that had just been sung, or which were to be sung following the playing of the piece. Thus, there is flexibility and freedom in terms of the registration you might choose for these pieces. However, it is best to remember some basic considerations, including no 16' reeds, judicious use of mixtures, and avoiding large-scale stops.

A Ground in Gamut — H. Purcell, 1659–1695
This piece is interesting as the "Ground" (which is the repeating bass line) is the same as that found in the Aria of Bach's Goldberg Variations. Did Bach know of this piece, or did he come across the melodic shape in some other form? As with the Voluntary, it is most appropriate to keep the registration simple. Flutes at 8' and 4' (and possible 2') would be ideal.

Fünf Variationen in F Major — G. F. Handel, 1685–1759
This piece is, fundamentally, a Chaconne. Customary performance practice would gradually increase the registration during the course of the piece. However, this piece is short enough that it could be played on a single registration, and it will still sound great. If you are to change registration between sections, you will need to add some additional time to allow for smooth changes. A little extra time will avoid scrambling and mishaps. That being said, the entire piece could be easily played on 8', 4', and 2' Flutes and sound convincing.

Toccata in G minor — G. F. Handel, 1685–1759
This is a lovely Toccata that can be played in a variety of different ways. Appearing in the "Postludes" section in the previous book, the intent of the editors is a large registration, perhaps a light Principal chorus, or a Flute chorus to 2'. It could, however, just as easily be played with an 8' and 2' flute to great effect.

Flight of Angels — G. F. Handel, 1685–1795
This piece was originally conceived for Musical Clock, a common device for composers to write for in the 17th and 18th centuries. Considering its provenance, therefore, keep the registration light and sparkling. Lots of upper work with only light mixtures. Experiment with including the Zymbelstern as you play (if you have one). It will add a lot to the overall effect!

Toccata — J. P. Sweelinck, 1562–1621
The organ Sweelinck played on was very limited in terms of stops and available colors. A simple registration of 8', 4', and 2' stops would preserve the fundamentally straighforward nature of the sound as Sweelinck would have conceived it.

Musette — F. Couperin, 1668–1733
Keep the registration bright. 8' and 2' Flutes would be perfect.

Ave Regina Coelorum — G. Dufay, c. 1400–1474
Try some different flute sounds for this piece. 8' alone or 8' and 4' together is a good choice. You can even try just a 4' flute on its own for a contrasting sound.

Ave Maria — W. E. Duncan, 1866–1920
This lovely prelude by a neglected English composer of beautiful music should be played on a soft selection of gentle flutes, at 8' only or 8' and 4' together.

Ave Maria — W. Byrd, 1540–1623
Originally written for voices, this piece is a lovely organ piece, and should be played on soft flutes, at 8' only or 8' and 4' together.

Ave Maris Stella — J. Dunstable, c. 1390–1453

This charming little miniature was written at a time when the organ was limited in tonal color and variety, and so it would be most appropriate to play it on a simple flute registration, either at 8' alone or at 8' and 4' pitch. As an alternative, you could try playing it on 4' flute alone. This can be an effective change to the usual 8' based registration.

Voluntary III — J. Stanley, 1712–1786

This calls for a bright Diapason with the addition of a 4' if you prefer.

Voluntary IX — Anonymous, XVIIIth c.

This calls for a bright Diapason with the addition of a 4' if you prefer.

Verset — L. J. A. Lefébure-Wély, 1817–1869

Wely says to use French Diapasons and flutes all at 8'. On Some American organs, if the Diapasons and flutes are thick-sounding, there is a technique — add 4' stops to better emulate the French sound.

Prélude pour le Kyrie de la Vierge — J.N. Lemmens, 1823–1881

This piece gives you two choices: 8', 4' 2' stops with a rich combinations of stops or even adding mutations and mixtures.

Voluntary VI — J. Stanley, 1712–1786

This calls for a bright Diapason with the addition of a 4' if you prefer.

Christ, God's Only Son — G. P. Telemann, 1681–1767

You may play this on Flute 8' and flute 2 2/3' on Swell or play Left Hand on the Swell with an 8' reed on the great.

Easy Organ Pieces from

The Catholic Organist's Quarterly

Painting of St. Cecilia by Circle of Ambrosius Benson

Fall

✦ Sacred Music Library ✦

THE VERDIN COMPANY

Elevation

Alexandre Guilmant, 1837–1911

Benedicamus Domino

Fughetta - Orbis Factor

Jacques-Nicolas Lemmens, 1823–1881

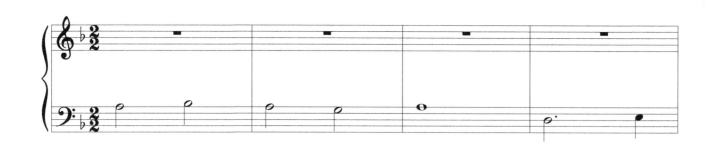

Toccata

Johann Christian Bach, 1735–1782

Thanks Be to God

Dank se Dir, Herr

Siegfried Ochs, 1858–1929

Von Himmel Hoch

From Heaven on High

Johann Gottfried Walther, 1684–1748

In Dulci Jubilo

Johann Michael Bach, 1648–1694

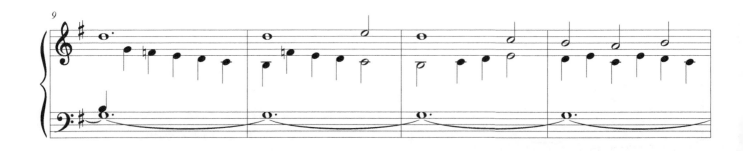

Ave Maris Stella

Chant Melody in Bass

François Benoist, 1794–1878

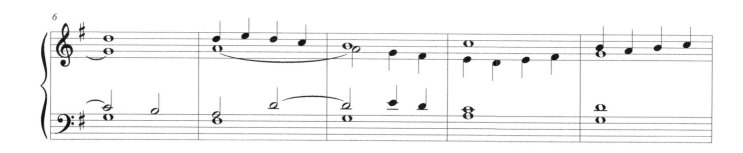

Easy Organ Pieces from

The Catholic Organist's Quarterly

Heilige Cäcilie - Joseph Anton Drägers - 1794-1833

Winter

✦ Sacred Music Library ✦

Grand Choeur

Hoc vos ô miseri – Himne pour le jour l'Épiphane
Poor wanderers, who make your prayer – Hymn for the day of Epiphany

Marc-Antoine Charpentier, 1643–1704

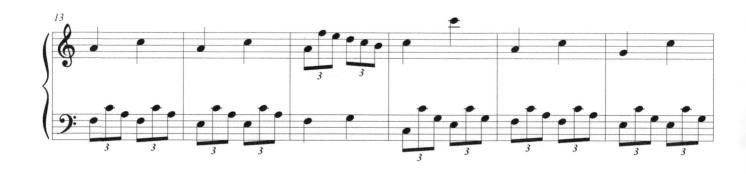

Quiet Prelude on MAGI

Noel Jones, b. 1947

[Chimes or other solo stop]

Da Jesus an dem Kreuze stund

Choralis in Cantu
Chorale in Soprano

Samuel Scheidt, 1587–1654

VI me Messe

Mass VI

Pour les Dimanches et les Fêtes dans le temps de Paques
For the Sundays and Feasts of Eastertide

Charles Justin, ca. 1830–ca. 1873

Asperges Me

Intonations for the Chant

Johann Diebold, 1842–1929

Kyrie Eleison

Lorenzo Perosi, 1872–1956

Regina Cæli

Queen of Heaven

Michel Corrette, 1707–1795

Antienne

Antiphon

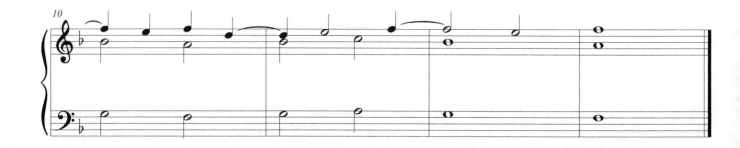

Grand Jeu
Full Organ

Amen

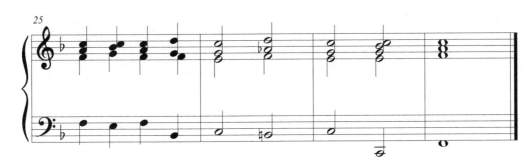

Rondeau

Jacques Duphly, 1715–1789

Cantilena

Oreste Ravanello, 1871–1938

Andantino Pastorale

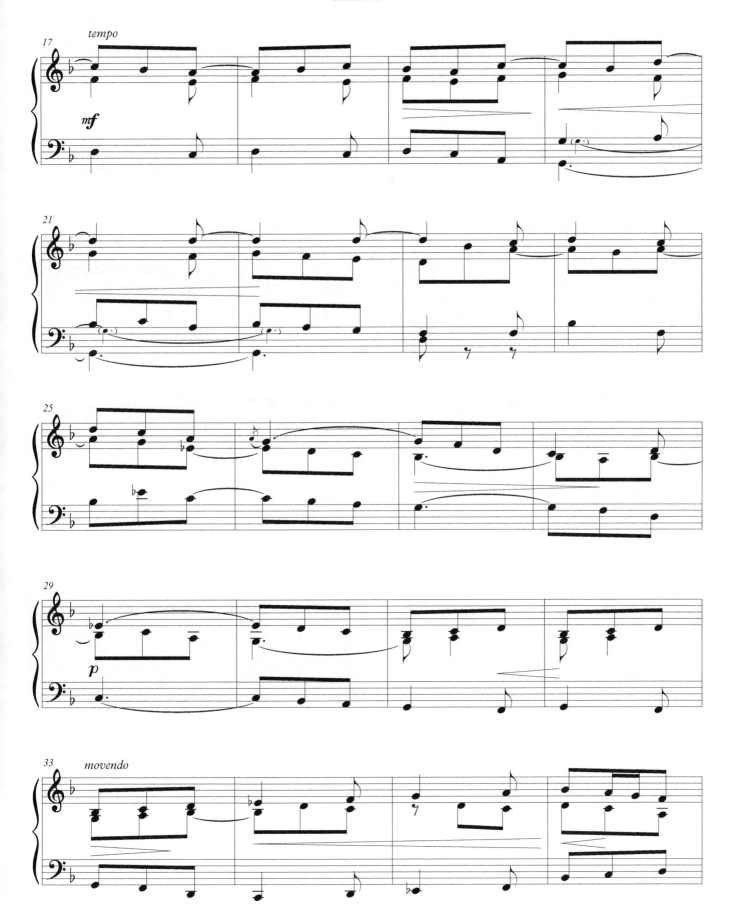

Vorspiel zu: Ecce Panis Angelorum

Introduction: Behold the Bread of Angels

Johann Diebold, 1842–1929

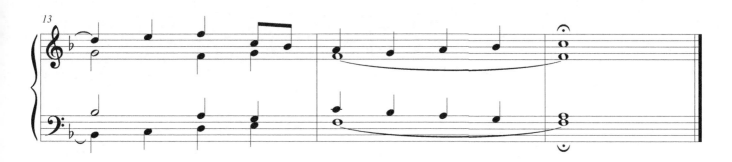

Benediction

Louis James Alfred Lefébure-Wély, 1817–1869

Andantino

Fughetta

Alessandro Scarlatti, 1660–1725

Fugue

Auguste Mathieu Panseron, 1756–1859

Fuga Sesta

Georg Philipp Telemann, 1681–1767

Basse de Trompette

Trumpet in Bass

Louis Marchand, 1669–1732

Rigaudon

Set as Trumpet Tune

Georg Böhm, 1661–1733
Arr. Noel Jones, b. 1947

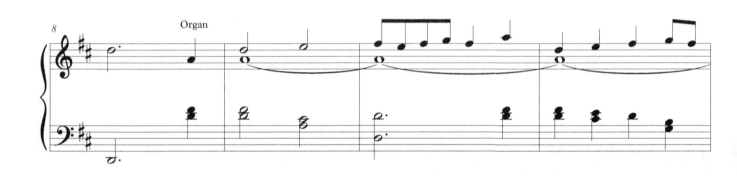

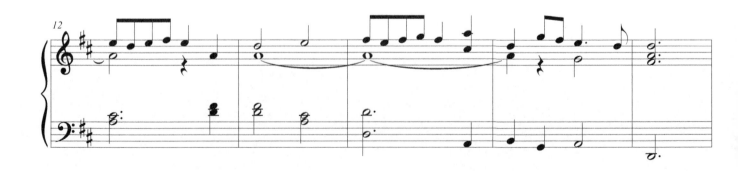

RH may be played an octave lower to X.

Easy Organ Pieces from

The Catholic Organist's Quarterly

Saint Cecilia • Edward Reginald Frampton · 1898

Spring

MANUALS ONLY

THE VERDIN COMPANY

Offertorio

del Secondo Tono

Jean-François Dandrieu, c. 1682–1738

Herr Jesu Christ dich zu uns wend

Lord Jesus Christ! Turn towards us

Georg Philipp Telemann, 1681–1767

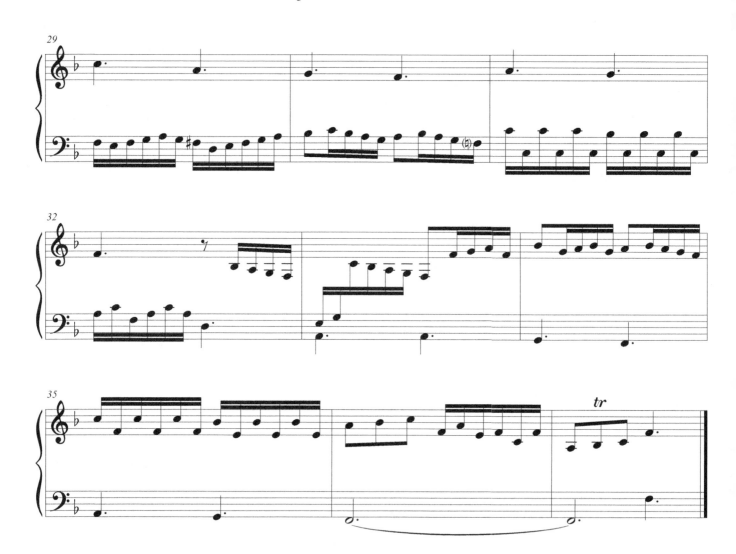

Basse de Trompette

Trumpet in the Bass

Jean-François Dandrieu, c. 1682–1738

Christ Ist Erstanden

Prelude

Buxheimer Orgelbuch, Completed 1460

Komm', Heiliger Geist

Come, Holy Ghost

Georg Philipp Telemann, 1681–1767

Veni Creator III

Jean Titelouze, 1563–1633

Easy Organ Pieces from

The Catholic Organist's Quarterly

Saint Cecilia, Edward Reginald Frampton, 1870–1923

Summer

MANUALS ONLY

THE VERDIN COMPANY

A Ground in Gamut

Henry Purcell, 1659–1695

Fünf Variationen in F Major

Ciacona con variazione

Georg Frideric Handel, 1685–1759

Toccata in G minor

Georg Frideric Handel, 1685–1759

Flight of Angels

HWV 600

Georg Frideric Handel, 1685–1795

Toccata

Jan Pieterszoon Sweelinck, 1562–1621

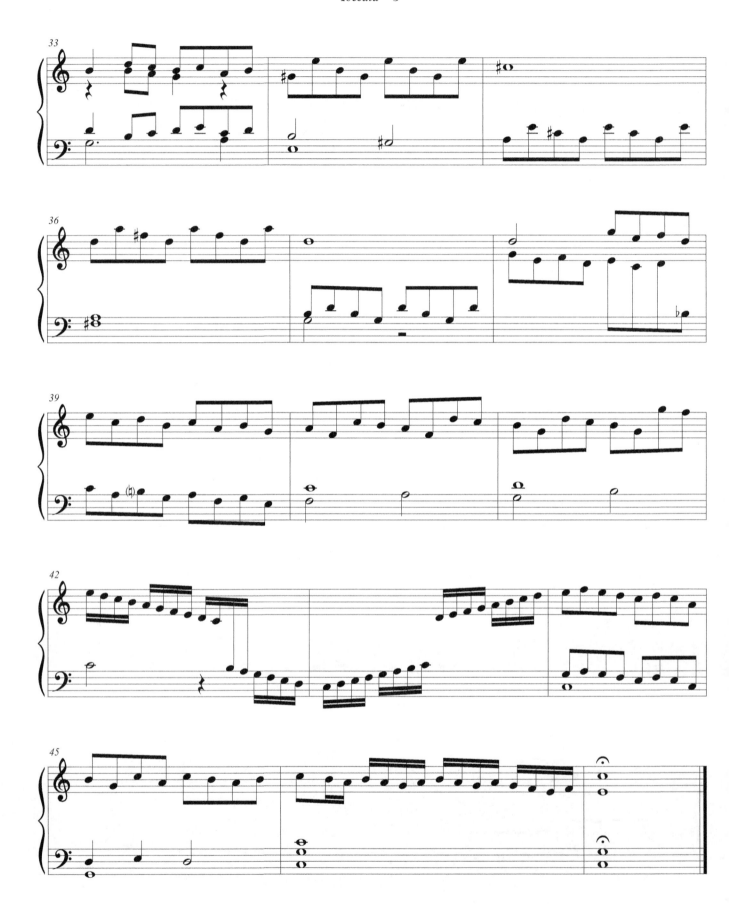

Musette

François Couperin, 1668–1733

Ave Regina Coelorum

Guillaume Dufay, c. 1400–1474

Easy Organ Pieces from

The Catholic Organist's Quarterly

St. Cecilia

Marian Organ Music
✦ Sacred Music Library ✦

Ave Maria

Introductory Voluntary

William Edmondstoune Duncan, 1866–1920

Ave Maria

William Byrd, 1540–1623

Ave Maris Stella

John Dunstable, c. 1390–1453

Easy Organ Pieces from

A Catholic Organist's Book of Preludes for Organ

Noel Jones, Editor • Sacred Music Library

Voluntary III

John Stanley, 1712–1786

Voluntary IX

Anonymous (XVIIIth c.)

Verset

L'Office Catholique, Op. 148

Montres et Flûtes de 8'

Louis James Alfred Lefébure-Wély, 1817–1869

Prelude pour le Kyrie de la Vierge

(2e Mode, transposé un ton plus haut)
École d'Orgue (1862)

Jacques-Nicolas Lemmens, 1823–1881

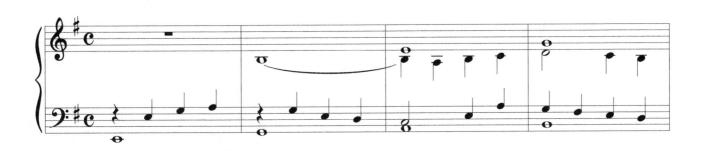

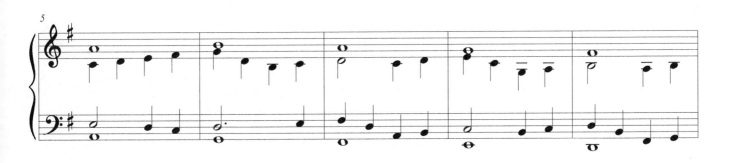

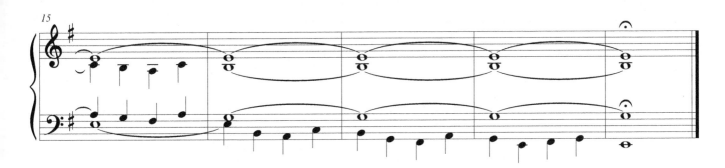

Easy Organ Pieces from

A Catholic Organist's Book of Offertory & Communion Music for Organ

Noel Jones, Editor • Sacred Music Library

Voluntary VI

John Stanley, 1712–1786

Christ, God's Only Son

Herr Christ der einig' Gottes Sohn

Georg Philipp Telemann, 1681–1767

EASY SHORT ORGAN PIECES IN EASY KEYS
IN ALPHABETICAL ORDER

Printed in Great Britain
by Amazon